A Collection of Australian Bush Verse

A. B. "BANJO" PATERSON

First published in Australia in 1993 by
Gary Allen Pty Ltd
9 Cooper Street
Smithfield NSW 2164

Designed and produced by Allan Cornwell
Typeset by The Craftsman Press
Produced by Mandarin Offset in Hong Kong

Photographs © Gary Lewis
ISBN 1-875169-39-3

LIST OF CONTENTS

INTRODUCTION

'The Banjo' was born Andrew Barton Paterson on 17 February 1841, at Narambla near Orange in New South Wales. The eldest child of Andrew Bogle Paterson and Rose Barton, he, his brother and five sisters lived with their parents on Illalong Station near Yass. During the first decade or so of his life, Paterson met many of the models for characters he would immortalise in his verse. The events of bush life surrounding him or recounted by friends, neighbours and acquaintances similarly were stored away for later use. Here, too, he began his long association with and admiration for horses.

Paterson was sent off to Sydney Grammar School at the age of ten, and matriculated six years later. He was then articled to a law firm and finally admitted as a solicitor. By the age of twenty-five he had already published 'Clancy of the Overflow' in the *Bulletin*, under his pseudonym 'The Banjo'. His father and sister Jessie also wrote poetry for the *Bulletin*, and his grandmother's verses circulated amongst some of the prominent cultural figures of her day.

The Man from Snowy River was published to enormous acclaim in 1895, and within a fortnight the first edition had sold out. By the end of its first year the book had sold over ten thousand copies, and more copies of it still sell than any other book of Australian poetry.

In the same year Paterson toured Queensland, visiting the stations of friends and ending up at Dagworth, a station some eighty kilometres north-west of Winton. Here he wrote the words of the best-known song in Australia – 'Waltzing Matilda' – which was set to a marching tune.

Banjo Paterson was a glamorous figure – handsome, strong and capable – whose life was full of travel and adventure. In the Northern Territory he hunted crocodiles and buffalo; he went pearling with the Japanese divers at Broome; and his journalism took him to the Boer War, to China to cover the Boxer Rebellion, and to the First World War. Unable to see any action in France, he soon resigned as war correspondent and became an ambulance driver for the Australian hospital at Wimereux. In 1916 he joined the Remount Service as a major, supplying horses to the Australian cavalry in the Middle East. His wife joined him in Egypt, and worked for the British Red Cross. He had married Alice Walker in 1903, and she, their daughter and son had lived periodically at Coodravale, their property on the upper Murrumbidgee.

After the war Alice and The Banjo returned to Sydney, where he took to journalism and writing again. Amongst the poems Paterson published in the Bulletin were several that debated the merits of bush life with Henry Lawson. Lawson took an altogether more lugubrious but also more sentimental view of the bush, stressing the hardships, loneliness and tragedies of country people. He accused Paterson of painting too cheerful a picture of the bush, of idealising the life and the people.

Paterson in turn accused Lawson of not having the stamina and spirit necessary for bush life. While acknowledging the hardships, he balanced them with the many beauties of the countryside and compared bush life favourably with the sordid, unhealthy squalor of city living.

Despite these differences of opinion, Paterson and Lawson shared much: both were nationalists, both were sympathetic with the workers and their politics, and both published in the then radical *Bulletin*. Unfortunately, the alcoholic Lawson ended his life in miserable circumstances, whereas Paterson was made CBE in the New Year honours of 1939, two years before his death at Sydney on 5 February 1941.

Today, the Banjo Paterson Award commemorates the writer and the region where he was born – every two years the Orange Festival of Arts makes the award for poetry and one-act plays. The Banjo inspired such works as Nigel Krauth's novel, *Matilda, My Darling*, and Clement Semmler's *The Banjo of the Bush: The Work, Life and Times of A. B. Paterson*.

Paterson's poetry was originally published in *The Man from Snowy River and Other Verses* (1895), *Rio Grande's Last Race and Other Verses* (1902), *Saltbush Bill J. P. and Other Verses* (1917) and *Collected Verse* (1923). The first and last of these are still immensely popular with Australians. Less well known is his prose: *An Outback Marriage* (1906) and *The Shearer's Colt* (1936), both novels, and *Three Elephant Power and Other Stories* (1917). He also wrote a book for children, *The Animals Noah Forgot* (1933). *Happy Dispatches* (1934), a semi-autobiographical work, included accounts of his adventures, and he compiled the anthology *Old Bush Songs* in 1905. His granddaughters collected all his writings and published them in two volumes: *Singer of the Bush and Song of the Pen.*

Our parents and grandparents knew many of Banjo Paterson's poems by heart, but today more people may know of the Man from Snowy River from the film than from the poem on which it is based. Paterson's verse has lost none of its power: the thrilling account of the ride down 'that terrible descent' is far more vivid and exciting than its celluloid offspring. And while fewer people today are familiar with the world that Paterson knew, his wit and humour are as fresh, and his characters as strong and unforgettable as ever.

THE MAN FROM SNOWY RIVER

THERE was movement at the station, for the word had passed around
That the colt from old Regret had got away,
And had joined the wild bush horses – he was worth a thousand
    pound,
So all the cracks had gathered to the fray.
All the tried and noted riders from the stations near and far
Had mustered at the homestead overnight,
For the bushmen love hard riding where the wild bush horses are,
And the stockhorse snuffs the battle with delight.

There was Harrison, who made his pile when Pardon won the cup,
The old man with his hair as white as snow;
But few could ride beside him when his blood was fairly up –
He would go wherever horse and man could go.
And Clancy of the Overflow came down to lend a hand,
No better horseman ever held the reins;
For never horse could throw him while the saddle girths would stand,
He learnt to ride while droving on the plains.

And one was there, a stripling on a small and weedy beast,
He was something like a racehorse undersized,
With a touch of Timor pony – three parts thoroughbred at least –
And such as are by mountain horsemen prized.
He was hard and tough and wiry – just the sort that won't say die –
There was courage in his quick impatient tread;
And he bore the badge of gameness in his bright and fiery eye,
And the proud and lofty carriage of his head.

But still so slight and weedy, one would doubt his power to stay,
And the old man said, "That horse will never do
For a long and tiring gallop – lad, you'd better stop away,
Those hills are far too rough for such as you."
So he waited sad and wistful – only Clancy stood his friend –
"I think we ought to let him come," he said;
"I warrant he'll be with us when he's wanted at the end,
For both his horse and he are mountain bred.

"He hails from Snowy River, up by Kosciusko's side,
Where the hills are twice as steep and twice as rough,
Where a horse's hoofs strike firelight from the flint stones every
    stride,
The man that holds his own is good enough.
And the Snowy River riders on the mountains make their home,
Where the river runs those giant hills between;
I have seen full many horsemen since I first commenced to roam,
But nowhere yet such horsemen have I seen."

So he went – they found the horses by the big mimosa clump –
They raced away towards the mountain's brow,
And the old man gave his orders, "Boys, go at them from the jump,
No use to try for fancy riding now.
And, Clancy, you must wheel them, try and wheel them to the right.
Ride boldly, lad, and never fear the spills,
For never yet was rider that could keep the mob in sight,
If once they gain the shelter of those hills."

So Clancy rode to wheel them – he was racing on the wing
Where the best and boldest riders take their place,
And he raced his stockhorse past them, and he made the ranges ring
With the stockwhip, as he met them face to face.

Then they halted for a moment, while he swung the dreaded lash,
But they saw their well-loved mountain full in view,
And they charged beneath the stockwhip with a sharp and sudden
    dash,
And off into the mountain scrub they flew.

Then fast the horsemen followed, where the gorges deep and black
Resounded to the thunder of their tread,
And the stockwhips woke the echoes, and they fiercely answered back
From cliffs and crags that beetled overhead.
And upward, ever upward, the wild horses held their way,
Where mountain ash and kurrajong grew wide;
And the old man muttered fiercely, "We may bid the mob good day,
No man can hold them down the other side."

When they reached the mountain's summit, even Clancy took a pull,
It well might make the boldest hold their breath,
The wild hop scrub grew thickly, and the hidden ground was full
Of wombat holes, and any slip was death.
But the man from Snowy River let the pony have his head,
And he swung his stockwhip round and gave a cheer,
And he raced him down the mountain like a torrent down its bed,
While the others stood and watched in very fear.

He sent the flint stones flying, but the pony kept his feet,
He cleared the fallen timber in his stride,
And the man from Snowy River never shifted in his seat –
It was grand to see that mountain horseman ride.
Through the stringybarks and saplings, on the rough and broken
    ground,
Down the hillside at a racing pace he went;
And he never drew the bridle till he landed safe and sound,
At the bottom of that terrible descent.

He was right among the horses as they climbed the further hill,
And the watchers on the mountain standing mute,
Saw him ply the stockwhip fiercely, he was right among them still,
As he raced across the clearing in pursuit.
Then they lost him for a moment, where two mountain gullies met
In the ranges, but a final glimpse reveals
On a dim and distant hillside the wild horses racing yet,
With the man from Snowy River at their heels.

And he ran them single-handed till their sides were white with foam.
He followed like a bloodhound on their track,
Till they halted cowed and beaten, then he turned their heads for
    home,
And alone and unassisted brought them back.
But his hardy mountain pony he could scarcely raise a trot,
He was blood from hip to shoulder from the spur;
But his pluck was still undaunted, and his courage fiery hot,
For never yet was mountain horse a cur.

And down by Kosciusko, where the pine-clad ridges raise
Their torn and rugged battlements on high,
Where the air is clear as crystal, and the white stars fairly blaze
At midnight in the cold and frosty sky,
And where around The Overflow the reed beds sweep and sway
To the breezes, and the rolling plains are wide,
The man from Snowy River is a household word today,
And the stockmen tell the story of his ride.

THE MAN FROM IRONBARK

IT was the man from Ironbark who struck the Sydney town,
He wandered over street and park, he wandered up and down.
He loitered here, he loitered there, till he was like to drop,
Until at last in sheer despair he sought a barber's shop.
"'Ere! shave my beard and whiskers off, I'll be a man of mark,
I'll go and do the Sydney toff up home in Ironbark."

The barber man was small and flash, as barbers mostly are,
He wore a strike-your-fancy sash, he smoked a huge cigar;
He was a humorist of note and keen at repartee,
He laid the odds and kept a "tote", whatever that may be,
And when he saw our friend arrive, he whispered, "Here's a lark!
Just watch me catch him all alive, this man from Ironbark."

There were some gilded youths that sat along the barber's wall.
Their eyes were dull, their heads were flat, they had no brains at all;
To them the barber passed the wink, his dexter eyelid shut,
"I'll make this bloomin' yokel think his bloomin' throat is cut."
And as he soaped and rubbed it in he made a rude remark:
"I s'pose the flats is pretty green up there in Ironbark."

A grunt was all reply he got; he shaved the bushman's chin,
Then made the water boiling hot and dipped the razor in.
He raised his hand, his brow grew black, he paused awhile to gloat,
Then slashed the red-hot razor-back across his victim's throat;
Upon the newly-shaven skin it made a livid mark –
No doubt it fairly took him in – the man from Ironbark.

He fetched a wild up-country yell might wake the dead to hear,
And though his throat, he knew full well, was cut from ear to ear,
He struggled gamely to his feet, and faced the murd'rous foe:
"You've done for me! you dog, I'm beat! one hit before I go!
I only wish I had a knife, you blessed murdering shark!
But you'll remember all your life the man from Ironbark."

He lifted up his hairy paw, with one tremendous clout
He landed on the barber's jaw, and knocked the barber out.
He set to work with nail and tooth, he made the place a wreck;
He grabbed the nearest gilded youth, and tried to break his neck.
And all the while his throat he held to save his vital spark,
And "Murder! Bloody murder!" yelled the man from Ironbark.

A peeler man who heard the din came into see the show;
He tried to run the bushman in, but he refused to go.
And when at last the barber spoke, and said "'Twas all in fun –
'Twas just a little harmless joke, a trifle overdone."
"A joke!" he cried, "By George, that's fine; a lively sort of lark;
I'd like to catch that murdering swine some night in Ironbark."

And now while round the shearing floor the list'ning shearers gape,
He tells the story o'er and o'er, and brags of his escape.
"Them barber chaps what keeps a tote, By George, I've had enough,
One tried to cut my bloomin' throat, but thank the Lord it's tough."
And whether he's believed or no, there's one thing to remark,
That flowing beards are all the go way up in Ironbark.

JOHNSON'S ANTIDOTE

DOWN along the Snakebite River, where the overlanders camp,
Where the serpents are in millions, all of the most deadly stamp;
Where the station cook in terror, nearly every time he bakes,
Mixes up among the doughboys half a dozen poison snakes:
Where the wily free selector walks in armour-plated pants,
And defies the stings of scorpions, and the bites of bulldog ants:
Where the adder and the viper tear each other by the throat,
There it was that William Johnson sought his snakebite antidote.

Johnson was a free selector, and his brain went rather queer,
For the constant sight of serpents filled him with a deadly fear;
So he tramped his free selection, morning, afternoon and night,
Seeking for some great specific that would cure the serpent's bite.
Till King Billy, of the Mooki, chieftain of the flour bag head,
Told him, "Spos'n snake bite pfeller, pfeller mostly drop down dead;
Spos'n snake bite old goanna, then you watch a while you see,
Old goanna cure himself with eating little pfeller tree."
"That's the cure," said William Johnson, "point me out this plant
    sublime",
But King Billy, feeling lazy, said he'd go another time.
Thus it came to pass that Johnson, having got the tale by rote,
Followed every stray goanna, seeking for the antidote.
                              ★   ★   ★   ★
Loafing once beside the river, while he thought his heart would break,
There he saw a big goanna, fighting with a tiger snake,
In and out they rolled and wriggled, bit each other, heart and soul,
Till the valiant old goanna swallowed his opponent whole.

Breathless, Johnson sat and watched him, saw him struggle up the
    bank,
Saw him nibbling at the branches of some bushes, green and rank;
Saw him, happy and contented, lick his lips, as off he crept,
While the bulging in his stomach showed where his opponent slept.
Then a cheer of exultation burst aloud from Johnson's throat;
"Luck at last," said he, "I've struck it! 'tis the famous antidote.

"Here it is, the Grand Elixir, greatest blessing ever known,
Twenty thousand men in India die each year of snakes alone.
Think of all the foreign nations, negro, chow, and blackamoor,
Saved from sudden expiration, by my wondrous snakebite cure.
It will bring me fame and fortune! In the happy days to be,
Men of every clime and nation will be round to gaze on me –
Scientific men in thousands, men of mark and men of note,
Rushing down the Mooki River, after Johnson's antidote.
It will cure *delirium tremens*, when the patient's eyeballs stare
At imaginary spiders, snakes which really are not there.
When he thinks he sees them wriggle, when he thinks he sees them
    bloat,
It will cure him just to think of Johnson's Snakebite Antidote."

Then he rushed to the museum, found a scientific man –
"Trot me out a deadly serpent, just the deadliest you can;
I intend to let him bite me, all the risk I will endure,
Just to prove the sterling value of my wondrous snakebite cure.
Even though an adder bit me, back to life again I'd float;
Snakes are out of date, I tell you, since I've found the antidote."
Said the scientific person, "If you really want to die,
Go ahead – but, if you're doubtful, let your sheepdog have a try.
Get a pair of dogs and try it, let the snake give both a nip;
Give your dog the snakebite mixture, let the other fellow rip;
If he dies and yours survives him, then it proves the thing is good.

Will you fetch your dog and try it?" Johnson rather thought he would
So he went and fetched his canine, hauled him forward by the throat.
"Stump, old man," says he, "we'll show them we've the genwine
    antidote."

Both the dogs were duly loaded with the poison gland's contents;
Johnson gave his dog the mixture, then sat down to wait events.
"Mark," he said, "in twenty minutes Stump'll be a-rushing round,
While the other wretched creature lies a corpse upon the ground."
But, alas for William Johnson! ere they'd watched a half-hour's spell
Stumpy was as dead as mutton, t'other dog was live and well.
And the scientific person hurried off with utmost speed,
Tested Johnson's drug and found it was a deadly poison weed;
Half a tumbler killed an emu, half a spoonful killed a goat,
All the snakes on earth were harmless to that awful antidote.

* * * *

Down along the Mooki River, on the overlanders' camp,
Where the serpents are in millions, all of the most deadly stamp,
Wanders, daily, William Johnson, down among those poisonous
    hordes,
Shooting every stray goanna, calls them "black and yaller frauds".
And King Billy, of the Mooki, cadging for the cast-off coat,
Somehow seems to dodge the subject of the snakebite antidote.

MULGA BILL'S BICYCLE

'Twas Mulga Bill, from Eaglehawk, that caught the cycling craze;
He turned away the good old horse that served him many days;
He dressed himself in cycling clothes, resplendent to be seen;
He hurried off to town and bought a shining new machine;
And as he wheeled it through the door, with air of lordly pride,
The grinning shop assistant said, "Excuse me, can you ride?"

"See here, young man," said Mulga Bill, "from Walgett to the sea,
From Conroy's Gap to Castlereagh, there's none can ride like me.
I'm good all round at everything, as everybody knows,
Although I'm not the one to talk – I *hate* a man that blows.
But riding is my special gift, my chiefest, sole delight;
Just ask a wild duck can it swim, a wildcat can it fight.
There's nothing clothed in hair or hide, or built of flesh or steel,
There's nothing walks or jumps, or runs, on axle, hoof, or wheel,
But what I'll sit, while hide will hold and girths and straps are tight:
I'll ride this here two-wheeled concern right straight away at sight."

'Twas Mulga Bill, from Eaglehawk, that sought his own abode,
That perched above the Dead Man's Creek, beside the mountain road.
He turned the cycle down the hill and mounted for the fray,
But ere he'd gone a dozen yards it bolted clean away.
It left the track, and through the trees, just like a silver streak,
It whistled down the awful slope towards the Dead Man's Creek.

It shaved a stump by half an inch, it dodged a big white-box:
The very wallaroos in fright went scrambling up the rocks,
The wombats hiding in their caves dug deeper underground,
As Mulga Bill, as white as chalk, sat tight to every bound.
It struck a stone and gave a spring that cleared a fallen tree,
It raced beside a precipice as close as close could be;
And then as Mulga Bill let out one last despairing shriek
It made a leap of twenty feet into the Dead Man's Creek.

'Twas Mulga Bill, from Eaglehawk, that slowly swam ashore:
He said, "I've had some narrer shaves and lively rides before;
I've rode a wild bull round a yard to win a five-pound bet,
But this was the most awful ride that I've encountered yet.
I'll give that two-wheeled outlaw best; it's shaken all my nerve
To feel it whistle through the air and plunge and buck and swerve.
It's safe at rest in Dead Man's Creek, we'll leave it lying still;
A horse's back is good enough henceforth for Mulga Bill."

OUT OF SIGHT

THEY held a polo meeting at a little country town,
And all the local sportsmen came to win themselves renown.
There came two strangers with a horse, and I am much afraid
They both belonged to what is called "the take-you-down brigade".

They said their horse could jump like fun, and asked an amateur
To ride him in the steeplechase, and told him they were sure,
The last time round, he'd sail away with such a swallow's flight
The rest would never see him go – he'd finish out of sight.

So out he went; and, when folk saw the amateur was up,
Some local genius called the race "the dude-in-danger cup".
The horse was known as "Who's Afraid", by "Panic" from
   "The Fright",
But still his owners told the jock he'd finish out of sight.

And so he did; for "Who's Afraid", without the least pretence,
Disposed of him by rushing through the very second fence;
And when they ran the last time round the prophecy was right –
For he was in the ambulance, and safely "out of sight".

CLANCY OF THE OVERFLOW

I had written him a letter which I had, for want of better
Knowledge, sent to where I met him down the Lachlan, years ago;
He was shearing when I knew him, so I sent the letter to him,
Just "on spec", addressed as follows: "Clancy, of The Overflow".

And an answer came directed in a writing unexpected,
(And I think the same was written with a thumbnail dipped in tar);
'Twas his shearing mate who wrote it, and *verbatim* I will quote it:
"Clancy's gone to Queensland droving, and we don't know where
   he are."

★ ★ ★ ★

In my wild erratic fancy visions come to me of Clancy
Gone a-droving "down the Cooper" where the western drovers go;
As the stock are slowly stringing, Clancy rides behind them singing,
For the drover's life has pleasures that the townsfolk never know.

And the bush hath friends to meet him, and their kindly voices
   greet him
In the murmur of the breezes and the river on its bars,
And he sees the vision splendid of the sunlit plains extended,
And at night the wondrous glory of the everlasting stars.

★ ★ ★ ★

I am sitting in my dingy little office, where a stingy
Ray of sunlight struggles feebly down between the houses tall,
And the foetid air and gritty of the dusty, dirty city
Through the open window floating, spreads its foulness over all.

And in place of lowing cattle, I can hear the fiendish rattle
Of the tramways and the buses making hurry down the street,
And the language uninviting of the gutter children fighting,
Comes fitfully and faintly through the ceaseless tramp of feet.

And the hurrying people daunt me, and their pallid faces haunt me
As they shoulder one another in their rush and nervous haste,
With their eager eyes and greedy, and their stunted forms and weedy,
For townsfolk have no time to grow, they have no time to waste.

And I somehow rather fancy that I'd like to change with Clancy,
Like to take a turn at droving where the seasons come and go,
While he faced the round eternal of the cashbook and the journal –
But I doubt he'd suit the office, Clancy, of "The Overflow".

A BUSH CHRISTENING

On the outer Barcoo where the churches are few,
And men of religion are scanty,
On a road never cross'd 'cept by folk that are lost,
One Michael Magee had a shanty.

Now this Mike was the dad of a ten-year-old lad,
Plump, healthy, and stoutly conditioned;
He was strong as the best, but poor Mike had no rest
For the youngster had never been christened.

And his wife used to cry, "If the darlin' should die
Saint Peter would not recognise him."
But by luck he survived till a preacher arrived,
Who agreed straightaway to baptise him.

Now the artful young rogue, while they held their collogue,
With his ear to the keyhole was listenin',
And he muttered in fright while his features turned white,
"What the divil and all is this christenin'?"

He was none of your dolts, he had seen them brand colts,
And it seemed to his small understanding,
If the man in the frock made him one of the flock,
It must mean something very like branding.

So away with a rush he set off for the bush,
While the tears in his eyelids they glistened –
"'Tis outrageous," says he, "to brand youngsters like me,
I'll be dashed if I'll stop to be christened!"

Like a young native dog he ran into a log,
And his father with language uncivil,
Never heeding the "praste" cried aloud in his haste,
"Come out and be christened, you divil!"

But he lay there as snug as a bug in a rug,
And his parents in vain might reprove him,
Till his reverence spoke (he was fond of a joke)
"I've a notion," says he, "that'll move him.

"Poke a stick up the log, give the spalpeen a prog;
Poke him aisy – don't hurt him or maim him,
'Tis not long that he'll stand, I've the water at hand,
As he rushes out this end I'll name him.

"Here he comes, and for shame! ye've forgotten the name –
Is it Patsy or Michael or Dinnis?"
Here the youngster ran out, and the priest gave a shout –
"Take your chance, anyhow, wid 'Maginnis'!"

As the howling young cub ran away to the scrub
Where he knew that pursuit would be risky,
The priest, as he fled, flung a flask at his head
That was labelled "Maginnis's Whisky!"

And Maginnis Magee has been made a J.P.,
And the one thing he hates more than sin is
To be asked by the folk who have heard of the joke,
How he came to be christened "Maginnis"!

SALTBUSH BILL

Now this is the law of the Overland that all in the West obey,
A man must cover with travelling sheep a six-mile stage a day;
But this is the law which the drovers make, right easily understood,
They travel their stage where the grass is bad, but they camp where
the grass is good;
They camp, and they ravage the squatter's grass till never a blade
remains,
Then they drift away as the white clouds drift on the edge of the
saltbush plains,
From camp to camp and from run to run they battle it hand to hand,
For a blade of grass and the right to pass on the track of the Overland.

For this is the law of the Great Stock Routes, 'tis written in white
and black –
The man that goes with a travelling mob must keep to a half-mile
track;
And the drovers keep to a half-mile track on the runs where the grass
is dead,
But they spread their sheep on a well-grassed run till they go with a
two-mile spread.
So the squatters hurry the drovers on from dawn till the fall of night,
And the squatters' dogs and the drovers' dogs get mixed in a deadly
fight;
Yet the squatters' men, though they hunt the mob, are willing the
peace to keep,
For the drovers learn how to use their hands when they go with the
travelling sheep;
But this is the tale of a Jackaroo that came from a foreign strand,
And the fight that he fought with Saltbush Bill, the King of the
Overland.

Now Saltbush Bill was a drover tough, as ever the country knew,

He had fought his way on the Great Stock Routes from the sea to the Big Barcoo;

He could tell when he came to a friendly run that gave him a chance to spread,

And he knew where the hungry owners were that hurried his sheep ahead;

He was drifting down in the Eighty drought with a mob that could scarcely creep,

(When the kangaroos by the thousands starve, it is rough on the travelling sheep.)

And he camped one night at the crossing place on the edge of the Wilga run,

"We must manage a feed for them here," he said, "or the half of the mob are done!"

So he spread them out when they left the camp wherever they liked to go,

Till he grew aware of a Jackaroo with a station hand in tow,

And they set to work on the straggling sheep, and with many a stockwhip crack

They forced them in where the grass was dead in the space of the half-mile track;

So William prayed that the hand of fate might suddenly strike him blue

But he'd get some grass for his starving sheep in the teeth of that Jackaroo.

So he turned and he cursed the Jackaroo, he cursed him alive or dead,

From the soles of his great unwieldy feet to the crown of his ugly head,

With an extra curse on the moke he rode and the cur at his heels that ran,

Till the Jackaroo from his horse got down and he went for the drover man;

With the station hand for his picker-up, though the sheep ran loose the
    while,
They battled it out on the saltbush plain in the regular prize ring style.

Now, the new chum fought for his honour's sake and the pride of the
    English race,
But the drover fought for his daily bread with a smile on his bearded
    face;
So he shifted ground and he sparred for wind and he made it a lengthy
    mill,
And from time to time as his scouts came in they whispered to
    Saltbush Bill –
"We have spread the sheep with a two-mile spread, and the grass it is
    something grand,
You must stick to him, Bill, for another round for the pride of the
    Overland."

The new chum made it a rushing fight, though never a blow got home,
Till the sun rode high in the cloudless sky and glared on the brick-red
    loam,
Till the sheep drew in to the shelter trees and settled them down to
    rest,
Then the drover said he would fight no more and he gave his opponent
    best.
So the new chum rode to the homestead straight and he told them a
    story grand
Of the desperate fight that he fought that day with the King of the
    Overland.
And the tale went home to the public schools of the pluck of the
    English swell,
How the drover fought for his very life, but blood in the end must tell.
But the travelling sheep and the Wilga sheep were boxed on the Old
    Man Plain.

'Twas a full week's work ere they drafted out and hunted them off
   again,
With a week's good grass in their wretched hides, with a curse and a
   stockwhip crack,
They hunted them off on the road once more to starve on the half-mile
   track.
And Saltbush Bill, on the Overland, will many a time recite,
How the best day's work that ever he did was the day that he lost the
   fight.

SHEARING AT CASTLEREAGH

The bell is set aringing, and the engine gives a toot,
There's five and thirty shearers here are shearing for the loot,
So stir yourselves, you penners-up and shove the sheep along,
The musterers are fetching them a hundred thousand strong,
And make your collie dogs speak up – what would the buyers say
In London if the wool was late this year from Castlereagh?

The man that "rung" the Tubbo shed is not the ringer here,
That stripling from the Cooma side can teach him how to shear.
They trim away the ragged locks, and rip the cutter goes,
And leaves a track of snowy fleece from brisket to the nose;
It's lovely how they peel it off with never stop nor stay,
They're racing for the ringer's place this year at Castlereagh.

The man that keeps the cutters sharp is growling in his cage,
He's always in a hurry and he's always in a rage –
"You clumsy-fisted muttonheads, you'd turn a fellow sick,
You pass yourselves as shearers? You were born to swing a pick!
Another broken cutter here, that's two you've broke today,
It's awful how such crawlers come to shear at Castlereagh."

The youngsters picking up the fleece enjoy the merry din,
They throw the classer up the fleece, he throws it to the bin;
The pressers standing by the rack are waiting for the wool,
There's room for just a couple more, the press is nearly full;
Now jump upon the lever, lads, and heave and heave away,
Another bale of golden fleece is branded "Castlereagh".

THE GEEBUNG POLO CLUB

It was somewhere up the country, in a land of rock and scrub,
That they formed an institution called the Geebung Polo Club.
They were long and wiry natives from the rugged mountain side,
And the horse was never saddled that the Geebungs couldn't ride;
But their style of playing polo was irregular and rash –
They had mighty little science, but a mighty lot of dash:
And they played on mountain ponies that were muscular and strong,
Though their coats were quite unpolished,
And their manes and tails were long.
And they used to train those ponies wheeling cattle in the scrub:
They were demons, were the members of the Geebung Polo Club.

It was somewhere down the country, in a city's smoke and steam,
That a polo club existed, called the Cuff and Collar Team.
As a social institution 'twas a marvellous success,
For the members were distinguished by exclusiveness and dress.
They had natty little ponies that were nice, and smooth, and sleek,
For their cultivated owners only rode 'em once a week.
So they started up the country in pursuit of sport and fame,
For they meant to show the Geebungs how they ought to play the
    game;
And they took their valets with them – just to give their boots a rub
Ere they started operations on the Geebung Polo Club.

Now my readers can imagine how the contest ebbed and flowed,
When the Geebung boys got going it was time to clear the road;
And the game was so terrific that ere half the time was gone
A spectator's leg was broken – just from merely looking on.

For they waddied one another till the plain was strewn with dead,
While the score was kept so even that they neither got ahead.
And the Cuff and Collar captain, when he tumbled off to die,
Was the last surviving player – so the game was called a tie.

Then the captain of the Geebungs raised him slowly from the ground,
Though his wounds were mostly mortal, yet he fiercely gazed around;
There was no one to oppose him – all the rest were in a trance,
So he scrambled on his pony for his last expiring chance,
For he meant to make an effort to get victory to his side;
So he struck at goal – and missed it – then he tumbled off and died.

★　★　★　★

By the old Campaspe River, where the breezes shake the grass,
There's a row of little gravestones that the stockmen never pass,
For they bear a crude inscription saying, "Stranger, drop a tear,
For the Cuff and Collar players and the Geebung boys lie here."
And on misty moonlit evenings, while the dingoes howl around,
You can see their shadows flitting down that phantom polo ground;
You can hear the loud collisions as the flying players meet,
And the rattle of the mallets, and the rush of ponies' feet,
Till the terrified spectator rides like blazes to the pub –
He's been haunted by the spectres of the Geebung Polo Club.

HOW GILBERT DIED

THERE'S never a stone at the sleeper's head,
There's never a fence beside,
And the wandering stock on the grave may tread
Unnoticed and undenied,
But the smallest child on the Watershed
Can tell you how Gilbert died.

For he rode at dusk, with his comrade Dunn
To the hut at the Stockman's Ford,
In the waning light of the sinking sun
They peered with a fierce accord.
They were outlaws both – and on each man's head
Was a thousand pounds reward.

They had taken toll of the country round,
And the troopers came behind
With a black that tracked like a human hound
In the scrub and the ranges blind:
He could run the trail where a white man's eye
No sign of a track could find.

He had hunted them out of the One Tree Hill
And over the Old Man Plain,
But they wheeled their tracks with a wild beast's skill,
And they made for the range again.
Then away to the hut where their grandsire dwelt,
They rode with a loosened rein.

And their grandsire gave them a greeting bold:
"Come in and rest in peace,
No safer place does the country hold –
With the night pursuit must cease,
And we'll drink success to the roving boys,
And to hell with the black police."

But they went to death when they entered there,
In the hut at the Stockman's Ford,
For their grandsire's words were as false as fair –
They were doomed to the hangman's cord.
He had sold them both to the black police
For the sake of the big reward.

In the depth of night there are forms that glide
As stealthy as serpents creep,
And around the hut where the outlaws hide
They plant in the shadows deep,
And they wait till the first faint flush of dawn
Shall waken their prey from sleep.

But Gilbert wakes while the night is dark –
A restless sleeper, aye,
He has heard the sound of a sheepdog's bark,
And his horse's warning neigh,
And he says to his mate, "There are hawks abroad,
And it's time that we went away."

Their rifles stood at the stretcher head,
Their bridles lay to hand,
They wakened the old man out of his bed,
When they heard the sharp command:
"In the name of the Queen lay down your arms,
Now, Dunn and Gilbert, stand!"

Then Gilbert reached for his rifle true
That close at his hand he kept,
He pointed it straight at the voice and drew,
But never a flash out leapt,
For the water ran from the rifle breach –
It was drenched while the outlaws slept.

Then he dropped the piece with a bitter oath,
And he turned to his comrade Dunn:
"We are sold," he said, "we are dead men both,
But there may be a chance for one;
I'll stop and I'll fight with the pistol here,
You take to your heels and run."

So Dunn crept out on his hands and knees
In the dim, half-dawning light,
And he made his way to a patch of trees,
And vanished among the night,
And the trackers hunted his tracks all day,
But they never could trace his flight.

But Gilbert walked from the open door
In a confident style and rash;
He heard at his side the rifles roar,
And he heard the bullets crash.
But he laughed as he lifted his pistol-hand,
And he fired at the rifle flash.

Then out of the shadows the troopers aimed
At his voice and the pistol sound,
With the rifle flashes the darkness flamed,
He staggered and spun around,
And they riddled his body with rifle balls
As it lay on the blood-soaked ground.

There's never a stone at the sleeper's head
There's never a fence beside,
And the wandering stock on the grave may tread
Unnoticed and undenied,
But the smallest child on the Watershed
Can tell you how Gilbert died.

LAST WEEK

OH, the new chum went to the backblock run,
But he should have gone there last week.
He tramped ten miles with a loaded gun,
But of turkey or duck he saw never a one,
For he should have been there last week,
   They said,
There were flocks of 'em there last week.

He wended his way to a waterfall,
And he should have gone there last week.
He carried a camera, legs and all,
But the day was hot, and the stream was small,
For he should have gone there last week,
   They said,
They drowned a man there last week.

He went for a drive, and he made a start,
Which should have been made last week,
For the old horse died of a broken heart;
So he footed it home and he dragged the cart –
But the horse was all right last week,
   They said,
He trotted a match last week.

So he asked the bushies who came from far
To visit the town last week,
If they'd dine with him, and they said, "Hurrah!"
But there wasn't a drop in the whisky jar –
"You should have been here last week,"
   He said,
"I drank it all up last week!"

HOW M'GINNIS WENT MISSING

LET us cease our idle chatter,
Let the tears bedew our cheek,
For a man from Tallangatta
Has been missing for a week.

Where the roaring, flooded Murray
Covered all the lower land,
There he started in a hurry,
With a bottle in his hand.

And his fate is hid for ever,
But the public seem to think
That he slumbered by the river,
'Neath the influence of drink.

And they scarcely seem to wonder
That the river, wide and deep,
Never woke him with its thunder,
Never stirred him in his sleep.

As the crashing logs came sweeping,
And their tumult filled the air,
Then M'Ginnis murmured, sleeping,
"'Tis a wake in ould Kildare."

So the river rose and found him
Sleeping softly by the stream,
And the cruel waters drowned him
Ere he wakened from his dream.

And the blossom-tufted wattle,
Blooming brightly on the lea
Saw M'Ginnis and the bottle
Going drifting out to sea.

WHEN DACEY RODE THE MULE

'TWAS in a small, up-country town,
When we were boys at school,
There came a circus with a clown
And with a bucking mule.
The clown announced a scheme they had –
The mule was such a king –
They'd give a crown to any lad
Who'd ride him round the ring.
And, gentle reader, do not scoff
Nor think the man a fool,
To buck a porous plaster off
Was pastime to that mule.

The boys got on – he bucked like sin –
He threw them in the dirt,
And then the clown would raise a grin
By asking, "Were they hurt?"
But Johnny Dacey came one night,
The crack of all the school,
Said he, "I'll win the crown all right,
Bring in your bucking mule."
The elephant went off his trunk,
The monkey played the fool
And all the band got blazing drunk
When Dacey rode the mule.

But soon there rose an awful shout
Of laughter, when the clown,
From somewhere in his pants drew out
A little paper crown.

He placed the crown on Dacey's head,
While Dacey looked a fool,
"Now, there's your crown, my lad," he said,
"For riding of the mule!"
The band struck up with "Killaloe",
And "Rule Britannia, Rule",
And "Young Man from the Country", too,
When Dacey rode the mule.

Then Dacey in a furious rage,
For vengeance on the show
Ascended to the monkeys' cage
And let the monkeys go;
The blue-tailed ape and chimpanzee
He turned abroad to roam;
Good faith! It was a sight to see
The people step for home.
For big baboons with canine snout
Are spiteful, as a rule,
The people didn't sit it out
When Dacey rode the mule.

And from the beasts that did escape
The bushmen all declare
Were born some creatures partly ape
And partly native bear.
They're rather few and far between;
The race is nearly spent;
But some of them may still be seen
In Sydney Parliament.
And when those legislators fight,
And drink, and act the fool –
It all commenced that wretched night
When Dacey rode the mule.

LAY OF THE MOTOR CAR

WE'RE away! and the wind whistles shrewd
In our whiskers and teeth;
And the granite-like grey of the road
Seems to slide underneath.
As an eagle might sweep through the sky,
So we sweep through the land;
And the pallid pedestrians fly
When they hear us at hand.

We outpace, we outlast, we outstrip!
Not the fast-fleeing hare,
Nor the racehorses under the whip,
Nor the birds of the air
Can compete with our swiftness sublime,
Our ease and our grace.
We annihilate chickens and time
And policemen and space.

Do you mind that fat grocer who crossed?
How he dropped down to pray
In the road when he saw he was lost;
How he melted away
Underneath, and there rang through the fog
His earsplitting squeal
As he went – is that he or a dog,
That stuff on the wheel?

SALTBUSH BILL'S SECOND FIGHT

THE news came down on the Castlereagh, and went to the world at
   large,
That twenty thousand travelling sheep, with Saltbush Bill in charge,
Were drifting down from a dried-out run to ravage the Castlereagh;
And the squatters swore when they heard the news, and wished they
   were well away:
For the name and the fame of Saltbush Bill were over the countryside
For the wonderful way that he fed his sheep, and the dodges and tricks
   he tried.
He would lose his way on a Main Stock Route, and stray to the
   squatters' grass;
He would come to a run with the boss away, and swear he had leave to
   pass;
And back of all and behind it all, as well the squatters knew,
If he had to fight, he would fight all day, so long as his sheep got
   through:
But this is the story of Stingy Smith, the owner of Hard Times Hill,
And the way that he chanced on a fighting man to reckon with
   Saltbush Bill.

                    ★ ★ ★ ★

'Twas Stingy Smith on his stockyard sat, and prayed for an early
   spring,
When he stared at sight of a clean-shaved tramp, who walked with
   jaunty swing;
For a clean-shaved tramp with a jaunty walk a-swinging along the
   track
Is as rare a thing as a feathered frog on the desolate roads outback.

So the tramp he made for the travellers' hut, and asked could he camp
  the night;
But Stingy Smith had a bright idea, and said to him, "Can you fight?"
"Why, what's the game?" said the clean-shaved tramp, as he looked at
  him up and down –
"If you want a battle, get off that fence, and I'll kill you for half-a-
  crown!
But, Boss, you'd better not fight with me, it wouldn't be fair nor right;
I'm Stiffener Joe, from the Rocks Brigade, and I killed a man in a
  fight:
I served two years for it, fair and square, and now I'm trampin' back,
To look for a peaceful quiet life away on the outside track –"
"Oh, it's not myself, but a drover chap," said Stingy Smith with glee;
"A bullying fellow, called Saltbush Bill – and you are the man for me.
He's on the road with his hungry sheep, and he's certain to raise a
  row,
For he's bullied the whole of the Castlereagh till he's got them under
  cow –
Just pick a quarrel and raise a fight, and leather him good and hard,
And I'll take good care that his wretched sheep don't wander a half a
  yard.
It's a five-pound job if you belt him well – do anything short of kill,
For there isn't a beak on the Castlereagh will fine you for Saltbush
  Bill."

"I'll take the job," said the fighting man, "and hot as this cove
  appears,
He'll stand no chance with a bloke like me, what's lived on the game
  for years:
For he's maybe learnt in a boxing school, and sparred for a round or
  so,
But I've fought all hands in a ten foot ring each night in a travelling
  show;

They earnt a pound if they stayed three rounds, and they tried for it
    every night –
In a ten foot ring! Oh, that's the game that teaches a bloke to fight,
For they'd rush and clinch, it was Dublin Rules, and we drew no
    colour line;
And they all tried hard for to earn the pound, but they got no pound of
    mine:
If I saw no chance in the opening round I'd slog at their wind, and
    wait
Till an opening came – and it *always* came – and I settled 'em, sure as
    fate;
Left on the ribs and right on the jaw – and, when the chance comes,
    make sure!
And it's there a professional bloke like me gets home on an amateur:

"For it's my experience every day, and I make no doubt it's yours,
That a third-class pro is an over-match for the best of the amateurs –"
"Oh, take your swag to the travellers' hut," said Smith, "for you waste
    your breath;
You've a first-class chance, if you lose the fight, of talking your man
    to death.
I'll tell the cook you're to have your grub, and see that you eat your
    fill,
And come to the scratch all fit and well to leather this Saltbush Bill."

★ ★ ★ ★

'Twas Saltbush Bill, and his travelling sheep were wending their
    weary way
On the Main Stock Route, through the Hard Times Run, on their six-
    mile stage a day;
And he strayed a mile from the Main Stock Route, and started to feed
    along,
And, when Stingy Smith came up, Bill said that the Route was
    surveyed wrong;

And he tried to prove that the sheep had rushed and strayed from their
    camp at night,
But the fighting man he kicked Bill's dog, and of course that meant a
    fight:

So they sparred and fought, and they shifted ground and never a sound
    was heard
But the thudding fists on their brawny ribs, and the seconds' muttered
    word,
Till the fighting man shot home his left on the ribs with a mighty
    clout,
And his right flashed up with a half-arm blow – and Saltbush Bill
    "went out".
He fell face down, and towards the blow; and their hearts with fear
    were filled,
For he lay as still as a fallen tree, and they thought that he must be
    killed.

So Stingy Smith and the fighting man, they lifted him from the
    ground,
And sent to home for a brandy flask, and they slowly fetched him
    round;
But his head was bad, and his jaw was hurt – in fact, he could scarcely
    speak –
So they let him spell till he got his wits, and he camped on the run a
    week,
While the travelling sheep went here and there, wherever they liked to
    stray,
Till Saltbush Bill was fit once more for the track to the Castlereagh.

             ★ ★ ★ ★

Then Stingy Smith he wrote a note, and gave to the fighting man:
'Twas writ to the boss of the neighbouring run, and thus the missive
    ran:
"The man with this is a fighting man, one Stiffener Joe by name;

He came near murdering Saltbush Bill, and I found it a costly game:
But it's worth your while to employ the chap, for there isn't the
    slightest doubt
You'll have no trouble from Saltbush Bill while this man hangs
    about –"
But an answer came by the next week's mail, with news that might
    well appal:
"The man you sent with a note is not a fighting man at all!
He has shaved his beard, and has cut his hair, but I spotted him at a
    look;
He is Tom Devine, who has worked for years for Saltbush Bill as
    cook.
Bill coached him up in the fighting yarn, and taught him the tale by
    rote,
And they shammed to fight, and they got your grass and divided your
    five-pound note.
'Twas a clean take-in, and you'll find it wise – 'twill save you a lot of
    pelf –
When next you're hiring a fighting man, just fight him a round
    yourself."
                      ★ ★ ★ ★
And the teamsters out on the Castlereagh, when they meet with a week
    of rain,
And the wagon sinks to its axle-tree, deep down in the black soil plain,
When the bullocks wade in a sea of mud, and strain at the load of
    wool,
And the cattle dogs at the bullocks' heels, are biting to make them
    pull,
When the offside driver flays the team, and curses them while he flogs,
And the air is thick with the language used, and the clamour of men
    and dogs –
The teamsters say, as they pause to rest and moisten each hairy throat,
They wish they could swear like Stingy Smith when he read that
    neighbour's note.

WALTZING MATILDA
(Carrying a Swag)

OH there once was a swagman camped in the billabongs,
Under the shade of a Coolibah tree;
And he sang as he looked at the old billy boiling,
"Who'll come a-waltzing Matilda with me."

CHORUS
Who'll come a-waltzing Matilda, my darling,
Who'll come a-waltzing Matilda with me.
Waltzing Matilda and leading a water-bag,
Who'll come a-waltzing Matilda with me.

Up came the jumbuck to drink at the waterhole,
Up jumped the swagman and grabbed him in glee;
And he sang as he put him away in his tucker-bag,
"You'll come a-waltzing Matilda with me."

CHORUS

Up came the squatter a-riding his thoroughbred;
Up came policemen – one, two, and three.
"Whose is the jumbuck you've got in the tucker-bag?
You'll come a-waltzing Matilda with me."

CHORUS

Up sprang the swagman and jumped in the waterhole,
Drowning himself by the Coolibah tree;
And his voice can be heard as it sings in the billabongs,
"Who'll come a-waltzing Matilda with me."

CHORUS

SALTBUSH BILL'S GAMECOCK

'TWAS Saltbush Bill, with his travelling sheep, was making his way to
    town;
He crossed them over the Hard Times Run, and he came to the Take
    'Em Down;
He counted through at the boundary gate, and camped at the drafting
    yard:
For Stingy Smith, of the Hard Times Run, had hunted him rather hard.
He bore no malice to Stingy Smith – 'twas simply the hand of fate
That caused his wagon to swerve aside and shatter old Stingy's gate;
And, being only the hand of fate, it follows, without a doubt,
It wasn't the fault of Saltbush Bill that Stingy's sheep got out.
So Saltbush Bill, with an easy heart, prepared for what might befall,
Commenced his stages on Take 'Em Down, the station of Rooster
    Hall.

'Tis strange how often the men outback will take to some curious
    craft,
Some ruling passion to keep their thoughts away from the overdraft;
And Rooster Hall, of the Take 'Em Down, was widely known to fame
As breeder of champion fighting cocks – his *forte* was the British
    Game.
The passing stranger within his gates that camped with old Rooster
    Hall
Was forced to talk about fowls all night, or else not talk at all.
Though droughts should come, and though sheep should die, his fowls
    were his sole delight
He left his shed in the flood of work to watch two gamecocks fight.

He held in scorn the Australian Game, that long-legged child of sin;
In a desperate fight, with the steel-tipped spurs, the British Game must
     win!
The Australian bird was a mongrel bird, with a touch of the jungle
     cock;
The want of breeding must find him out, when facing the English
     stock;
For British breeding, and British pluck, must triumph it over all–
And that was the root of the simple creed that governed old Rooster
     Hall.

* * * *

'Twas Saltbush Bill to the station rode ahead of his travelling sheep,
And sent a message to Rooster Hall that wakened him out of his
     sleep –
A crafty message that fetched him out, and hurried him as he came –
"A drover has an Australian Bird to match with your British Game."
'Twas done, and done in half a trice; a five-pound note aside;
Old Rooster Hall, with his champion bird, and the drover's bird
     untried.
"Steel spurs, of course?" said old Rooster Hall; "you'll need 'em,
     without a doubt!"
"You stick the spurs on your bird," said Bill, "but mine fights best
     without."
"Fights best without?" said old Rooster Hall; "he can't fight best
     unspurred!
You must be crazy!" But Saltbush Bill said, "Wait till you see my
     bird!"
So Rooster Hall to his fowl yard went, and quickly back he came,
Bearing a clipt and a shaven cock, the pride of his English Game.
With an eye as fierce as an eaglehawk, and a crow like a trumpet call,
He strutted about on the garden walk, and cackled at Rooster Hall.

Then Rooster Hall sent off a boy with word to his cronies two,
McCrae (the boss of the Black Police) and Father Donahoo.
Full many a cockfight old McCrae had held in his empty Court,
With Father D. as a picker-up – a regular all-round Sport!
They got the message of Rooster Hall, and down to his run they came,
Prepared to scoff at the drover's bird, and to bet on the English Game;
They hied them off to the drover's camp, while Saltbush rode before –
Old Rooster Hall was a blithesome man, when he thought of the treat in store.
They reached the camp, where the drover's cook, with countenance all serene,
Was boiling beef in an iron pot, but never a fowl was seen.

"Take off the beef from the fire," said Bill, "and wait till you see the fight;
There's something fresh for the bill-of-fare – there's game-fowl stew to-night!
For Mister Hall has a fighting cock, all feathered and clipped and spurred;
And he's fetched him here, for a bit of sport, to fight our Australian bird.
I've made a match that our pet will win, though he's hardly a fighting cock,
But he's game enough, and it's many a mile that he's tramped with the travelling stock."
The cook he banged on a saucepan lid; and , soon as the sound was heard,
Under the dray, in the shadows hid, a something moved and stirred:
A great tame Emu strutted out. Said Saltbush, "Here's our bird!"
But Rooster Hall, and his cronies two, drove home without a word.

The passing stranger within his gates that camps with old Rooster Hall
Must talk about something else than fowls, if he wishes to talk at all.
For the record lies in the local Court, and filed in its deepest vault,
That Peter Hall, of the Take 'Em Down, was tried for a fierce assault
On a stranger man, who, in all good faith, and prompted by what he
heard,
Had asked old Hall if a British Game could beat an Australian bird;
And old McCrae, who was on the Bench, as soon as the case was
tried,
Remarked, "Discharged with a clean discharge – the assault was
justified!"

PIONEERS

THEY came of bold and roving stock that would not fixed abide;
They were the sons of field and flock since e'er they learned to ride;
We may not hope to see such men in these degenerate years
As those explorers of the bush – the brave old pioneers.

'Twas they who rode the trackless bush in heat and storm and drought;
'Twas they that heard the master-word that called them further out;
'Twas they that followed up the trail the mountain cattle made
And pressed across the mighty range where now their bones are laid.

But now the times are dull and slow, the brave old days are dead
When hardy bushmen started out, and forced their way ahead
By tangled scrub and forests grim towards the unknown west,
And spied the far-off promised land from off the ranges' crest.

Oh! ye, that sleep in lonely graves by far-off ridge and plain,
We drink to you in silence now as Christmas comes again,
The men who fought the wilderness through rough, unsettled years –
The founders of our nation's life, the brave old pioneers.

A WALGETT EPISODE

The sun strikes down with a blinding glare,
The skies are blue and the plains are wide,
The saltbush plains that are burnt and bare
By Walgett out on the Barwon side –
The Barwon River that wanders down
In a leisurely manner by Walgett Town.

There came a stranger – a "cockatoo" –
The word means farmer, as all men know
Who dwell in the land where the kangaroo
Barks loud at dawn, and the white-eyed crow
Uplifts his song on the stockyard fence
As he watches the lambkins passing hence.

The sunburnt stranger was gaunt and brown,
But it soon appeared that he meant to flout
The iron law of the country town,
Which is – that the stranger has got to shout:
"If he will not shout we must take him down,"
Remarked the yokels of Walgett Town.

They baited a trap with a crafty bait,
With a crafty bait, for they held discourse
Concerning a new chum who of late
Had bought such a thoroughly lazy horse;
They would wager that no one could ride him down
The length of the city of Walgett Town.

The stranger was born on a horse's hide;
So he took the wagers, and made them good
With his hard-earned cash – but his hopes they died,
For the horse was a clothes-horse, made of wood!
'Twas a well-known horse that had taken down
Full many a stranger in Walgett Town.

The stranger smiled with a sickly smile –
'Tis a sickly smile that the loser grins –
And he said he had travelled for quite a while
In trying to sell some marsupial skins.
"And I thought that perhaps, as you've took me down,
You would buy them from me, in Walgett Town!"

He said that his home was at Wingadee,
At Wingadee where he had for sale
Some fifty skins and would guarantee
They were full-sized skins, with the ears and tail
Complete, and he sold them for money down
To a venturesome buyer in Walgett Town.

Then he smiled a smile as he pouched the pelf,
"I'm glad that I'm quit of them, win or lose:
You can fetch them in when it suits yourself,
And you'll find the skins – on the kangaroos!!"
Then he left – and the silence settled down
Like a tangible thing upon Walgett Town.

BEEN THERE BEFORE

THERE came a stranger to Walgett town,
To Walgett town when the sun was low,
And he carried a thirst that was worth a crown,
Yet how to quench it he did not know;
But he thought he might take those yokels down,
The guileless yokels of Walgett town.

They made him a bet in a private bar,
In a private bar when the talk was high,
And they bet him some pounds no matter how far
He could pelt a stone, yet he could not shy
A stone right over the river so brown,
The Darling River at Walgett town.

He knew that the river from bank to bank
Was fifty yards, and he smiled a smile
As he trundled down, but his hopes they sank
For there wasn't a stone within fifty mile;
For the saltbush plain and the open down
Produce no quarries in Walgett town.

The yokels laughed at his hopes o'erthrown,
And he stood awhile like a man in a dream;
Then out of his pocket he fetched a stone,
And pelted it over the silent stream –
He had been there before: he had wandered down
On a previous visit to Walgett town.

THE RIDERS IN THE STAND

THERE'S some that ride the Robbo style, and bump at every stride;
While others sit a long way back, to get a longer ride.
There's some that ride like sailors do, with legs, and arms, and teeth;
And some ride on the horse's neck, and some ride underneath.

But all the finest horsemen out – the men to beat the band –
You'll find amongst the crowd that ride their races in the stand.
They'll say, "He had the race in hand, and lost it in the straight".
They'll show how Godby came too soon,and Barden came too late.

They'll say Chevalley lost his nerve, and Regan lost his head;
They'll tell how one was "livened up" and something else was
   "dead" –
In fact, the race was never run on sea, or sky, or land,
But what you'd get it better done by riders in the stand.

The rule holds good in everything in life's uncertain fight:
You'll find the winner can't go wrong, the loser can't go right.
You ride a slashing race, and lose – by one and all you're banned!
Ride like a bag of flour, and win – they'll cheer you in the stand.

FATHER RILEY'S HORSE

'TWAS the horse thief, Andy Regan, that was hunted like a dog
By the troopers of the upper Murray side,
They had searched in every gully – they had looked in every log,
But never sight or track of him they spied,
Till the priest at Kiley's Crossing heard a knocking very late
And a whisper "Father Riley – come across!"
So his Rev'rence in pyjamas trotted softly to the gate
And admitted Andy Regan – and a horse!

"Now, it's listen, Father Riley, to the words I've got to say,
For it's close upon my death I am tonight.
With the troopers hard behind me I've been hiding all the day
In the gullies keeping close and out of sight.
But they're watching all the ranges till there's not a bird could fly,
And I'm fairly worn to pieces with the strife,
So I'm taking no more trouble, but I'm going home to die,
'Tis the only way I see to save my life.

"Yes, I'm making home to mother's and I'll die o'Tuesday next
An' be buried on theThursday – and, of course,
I'm prepared to meet my penance, but with one thing I'm perplexed
And it's – Father, it's this jewel of a horse!
He was never bought nor paid for, and there's not a man can swear
To his owner or his breeder, but I know,
That his sire was by Pedantic from the Old Pretender mare
And his dam was close related to The Roe.

"And there's nothing in the district that can race him for a step,
He could canter while they're going at their top:
He's the king of all the leppers that was ever seen to lep,
A five-foot fence – he'd clear it in a hop!
So I'll leave him with you, Father, till the dead shall rise again,
'Tis yourself that knows a good 'un; and, of course,
You can say he's got by Moonlight out of Paddy Murphy's plain
If you're ever asked the breeding of the horse!

"But it's getting on to daylight and it's time to say goodbye,
For the stars above the east are growing pale.
And I'm making home to mother – and it's hard for me to die!
But it's harder still, is keeping out of gaol!
You can ride the old horse over to my grave across the dip
Where the wattle bloom is waving overhead.
Sure he'll jump them fences easy – you must never raise the whip
Or he'll rush 'em! – now, goodbye!" and he had fled!

So they buried Andy Regan, and they buried him to rights,
In the graveyard at the back of Kiley's Hill;
There were five-and-twenty mourners who had five-and-twenty fights
Till the very boldest fighters had their fill.
There were fifty horses racing from the graveyard to the pub,
And their riders flogged each other all the while.
And the lashin's of the liquor! And the lavin's of the grub!
Oh, poor Andy went to rest in proper style.

Then the races came to Kiley's – with a steeplechase and all,
For the folk were mostly Irish round about,
And it takes an Irish rider to be fearless of a fall,
They were training morning in and morning out.

But they never started training till the sun was on the course
For a superstitious story kept 'em back,
That the ghost of Andy Regan on a slashing chestnut horse,
Had been training by the starlight on the track.

And they read the nominations for the races with surprise
And amusement at the Father's little joke,
For a novice had been entered for the steeplechasing prize,
And they found that it was Father Riley's moke!
He was neat enough to gallop, he was strong enough to stay!
But his owner's views of training were immense,
For the Reverend Father Riley used to ride him every day,
And he never saw a hurdle nor a fence.

And the priest would join the laughter: "Oh," said he, "I put him in,
For there's five-and-twenty sovereigns to be won.
And the poor would find it useful, if the chestnut chanced to win,
And he'll maybe win when all is said and done!"
He had called him Faugh-a-ballagh, which is French for "clear the
    course",
And his colours were a vivid shade of green:
All the Dooleys and O'Donnells were on Father Riley's horse,
While the Orangemen were backing Mandarin!

It was Hogan, the dog poisoner – aged man and very wise,
Who was camping in the racecourse with his swag,
And who ventured the opinion, to the township's great surprise,
That the race would go to Father Riley's nag.
"You can talk about your riders – and the horse has not been schooled,
And the fences is terrific, and the rest!
When the field is fairly going, then ye'll see ye've all been fooled,
And the chestnut horse will battle with the best.

"For there's some has got condition, and they think the race is sure,
And the chestnut horse will fall beneath the weight,
But the hopes of all the helpless, and the prayers of all the poor,
Will be running by his side to keep him straight.
And it's what's the need of schoolin' or of workin' on the track,
Whin the saints are there to guide him round the course!
I've prayed him over every fence – I've prayed him out and back!
And I'll bet my cash on Father Riley's horse!"

* * * *

Oh, the steeple was a caution! They went tearin' round and round,
And the fences rang and rattled where they struck.
There was some that cleared the water –there was more fell in and
    drowned,
Some blamed the men and others blamed the luck!
But the whips were flying freely when the field came into view,
For the finish down the long green stretch of course,
And in front of all the flyers – jumpin' like a kangaroo,
Came the rank outsider – Father Riley's horse!

Oh, the shouting and the cheering as he rattled past the post!
For he left the others standing, in the straight;
And the rider – well, they reckoned it was Andy Regan's ghost,
And it beat 'em how a ghost would draw the weight!
But he weighed in, nine stone seven, then he laughed and disappeared,
Like a banshee (which is Spanish for an elf),
And old Hogan muttered sagely, "If it wasn't for the beard
They'd be thinking it was Andy Regan's self!"

And the poor of Kiley's Crossing drank the health at Christmastide
Of the chestnut and his rider dressed in green.
There was never such a rider, not since Andy Regan died,
And they wondered who on earth he could have been.
But they settled it among 'em, for the story got about,
'Mongst the bushmen and the people on the course,
That the Devil had been ordered to let Andy Regan out
For the steeplechase on Father Riley's horse!

AS LONG AS YOUR EYES ARE BLUE

WILT thou love me, sweet, when my hair is grey,
And my cheeks shall have lost their hue?
When the charms of youth shall have passed away,
Will your love as of old prove true?
For the looks may change, and the heart may range,
And the love be no longer fond;
Wilt thou love with truth in the years of youth
And away to the years beyond?

Oh, I love you, sweet, for your locks of brown
And the blush on your cheek that lies –
But I love you most for the kindly heart
That I see in your sweet blue eyes –
For the eyes are signs of the soul within,
Of the heart that is real and true,
And mine own sweetheart, I shall love you still,
Just as long as your eyes are blue.

For the locks may bleach, and the cheeks of peach
May be reft of their golden hue;
But mine own sweetheart, I shall love you still,
Just as long as your eyes are blue.

DO THEY KNOW?

Do they know? At the turn to the straight
Where the favourites fail,
And every atom of weight
Is telling its tale;
As some grim old stayer hard-pressed
Runs true to his breed,
And with head just in front of the rest
Fights on in the lead;
When the jockeys are out with the whips,
With a furlong to go;
And the backers grow white to the lips –
Do you think *they* don't know?

Do they know? As they come back to weigh
In a whirlwind of cheers,
Though the spurs have left marks of the fray,
Though the sweat on the ears
Gathers cold, and they sob with distress
As they roll up the track,
They know just as well their success
As the man on their back.
As they walk through a dense human lane,
That sways to and fro,
And cheers them again and again,
Do you think *they* don't know?

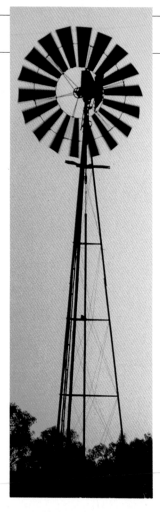

PHOTOGRAPHY BY GARY LEWIS